Who Was
Leif Erikson?

by Nico Medina

illustrated by Dede Putra

Penguin Workshop
An Imprint of Penguin Random House

In memory of my grandmother Iris "Johansson"
Kupfer, gifted pianist and inspiring Viking
woman—NM

PENGUIN WORKSHOP
Penguin Young Readers Group
An Imprint of Penguin Random House LLC

Text copyright © 2018 by Nico Medina. Illustrations copyright © 2018 by
Penguin Random House LLC. All rights reserved. Published by Penguin Workshop,
an imprint of Penguin Random House LLC, 345 Hudson Street, New York,
New York 10014. PENGUIN and PENGUIN WORKSHOP are trademarks of
Penguin Books Ltd. WHO HQ & Design is a registered trademark of
Penguin Random House LLC. Printed in the USA.

Library of Congress Cataloging-in-Publication Data is available.

ISBN 9780448488615 (paperback)   10 9 8 7 6 5 4 3 2 1
ISBN 9781524786731 (library binding)   10 9 8 7 6 5 4 3 2 1

Contents

Who Was Leif Erikson? 1

Erik's Son 6

Greenland 18

Life of a Viking 27

The Viking Way of War 44

The Viking Age 54

The Road to Valhalla 65

Voyage to Vinland 78

The Vikings and the Skraelings 89

Life After Leif 98

Timelines 106

Bibliography 108

Who Was Leif Erikson?

Leif Erikson (say: LEEF AY-rick-sun) was only around twenty years old. But he had already accomplished quite a bit in his young life. And now, in the year 1000, he was sailing across the stormy North Atlantic Ocean from his home in Greenland to visit the king of Norway. It was a journey of several days. When Leif arrived in Norway, King Olaf was happy to meet him.

During their visit, Olaf and Leif talked about a friend of Leif's, Bjarni Herjólfsson (say: bih-YAR-nee hair-YOLF-sun). Bjarni had visited with King Olaf a couple of years earlier and had told him a story Leif knew well, about a mysterious land that lay west of Greenland.

Bjarni had spotted this heavily forested land on an earlier sea voyage. He had been sailing to Greenland but became lost when his ship was blown off course. An unfamiliar coast came into view. Bjarni's crew asked if they could go ashore to explore, but Bjarni was too cautious. He didn't want to put the crew in any danger. He refused.

King Olaf and his friends told Bjarni that he should have listened to his crew! And they now told Leif that they thought Bjarni had missed a once-in-a-lifetime opportunity.

Leif wondered: Could there *really* be an unknown and unexplored land west of Greenland?

The folk stories of Norse mythology, the

original religion of his youth, had taught Leif that the world he lived in was flat. He believed that the border of this flat area was encircled by a terrible snake-monster. And if you sailed too far from home, you might come face-to-face with it—and meet a terrifying end!

But maybe there was more to the world than his mythology had taught him.

Leif was determined to return to Greenland and attempt to do what Bjarni hadn't: explore this mysterious New World. Just as his father, Erik the Red, had done in Greenland, Leif wanted to build a Viking settlement where no one had dared to before.

Leif Erikson would soon become the first European to set foot on North America—more than four hundred years before Christopher Columbus was even born!

CHAPTER 1
Erik's Son

Leif Erikson was born in Iceland around the year 980. His last name, Erikson (or "Erik's son"), came from his father, Erik Thorvaldsson, called Erik the Red. Like many Vikings before him, Leif was born into a life of exploration and adventure.

Erik the Red

Erik the Red had grown up in Norway, nine hundred miles away from Iceland. He got his name from his fiery red hair and beard—and his violent temper.

When Erik the Red was about ten years old, his father, Leif's grandfather, committed a murder. The king of Norway banished Erik and his father—he forced them to leave the country.

Viking kings, like the king of Norway, were very powerful men. Their history began with King Harald about one hundred years earlier.

Harald Fairhair, the First King of Norway
(c. 850–933)

Before King Harald, Norway was a collection of smaller kingdoms ruled by chieftains—the heads of the local clans or tribes. When Harald was just ten years old, he became ruler of the kingdom of Vestfold. Years later, the legends say, he proposed to Princess Gyda. But Gyda said that she would not marry Harald until he had a great kingdom like Erik Anundsson of Sweden, or Gorm the Old of Denmark, two men who had recently united their countries. Harald vowed to unite the clans of Norway. He also promised that until he had done so, he would not cut or comb his hair!

Over the next ten years, Harald conquered kingdom after kingdom. He allowed the local chieftains to stay in power, as long as they paid taxes and sent men to Norway's national army. Victory was his! Harald finally cut his wild and tangled hair. His handsome new look earned him his nickname, Fairhair. He and Gyda married. King Harald Fairhair would rule Norway for more than fifty years.

Today, buried in the cliffs above the site of his final battle, stands a monument of three Viking swords commemorating King Harald and the birthplace of modern Norway.

Erik the Red and his father left Norway and sailed to their new home: Iceland. Erik grew up and eventually purchased a sheep farm and married his wife, Thjodhild (say: JODE-hiled). They had three sons, Thorvald, Leif, and Thorstein. Leif also had a sister named Freydis. Erik and Thjodhild's children belonged to a typical Viking family.

The Vikings were fierce warriors and sailors from Norway, Denmark, and Sweden—the lands together known as Scandinavia. Since the late 700s, whenever summer rolled around, the Vikings left their homes in Scandinavia seeking adventure, glory, and treasure in lands across Europe. They were pirates who took what they wanted from the people they conquered, including other people whom they used as slaves. Many Vikings settled in the new lands they attacked, from England to Ireland to Iceland—and as far away as Greenland.

In the summers, Erik the Red and his men sailed away in search of villages to threaten. In these violent and deadly raids, Erik and his fellow Viking warriors burned villages to the ground and stole anything of value. The Vikings had been doing this for hundreds of years, all around Europe. Villagers who weren't killed might be taken as slaves.

Erik the Red owned slaves in Iceland. One day, the slaves caused a rockslide, which damaged Erik's neighbor's house. It was an accident, but the neighbor reacted violently, by killing Erik's slaves.

Erik responded with a violent attack of his own: by killing his neighbor—and his neighbor's cousin!

Charges were brought against Erik at the Thing.

Here's the Thing . . .

The Thing was a meeting of Viking townspeople where disputes were settled and laws were made. Crime and punishment were discussed.

The Thing was a meeting run by the local chieftain. There was also a "law speaker" who recited the laws from memory, since there was no written record of them. The chieftain and law speaker made

the decisions, but all freemen at the Thing were welcome to offer their opinions. Women could attend the Thing but were not allowed to speak.

Larger regional and national Thing meetings took place at certain times of the year. The Icelandic national Thing met for the first time around 930. It is the oldest form of parliament in Europe!

The Thing reached its decision: Erik the Red was declared an outlaw. Like his father before him in Norway, Erik was banished. He would have to leave Iceland immediately. Even worse, Erik's fellow Icelanders were allowed to kill him if he didn't hurry up!

Luckily, Erik had a few friends left in Iceland. They helped hide him while he prepared his family, his ship, and his crew to set sail. But where would he go?

He could never return to Norway. Nor to Ireland or England, which had become crowded with too many other Viking settlers.

Erik decided to sail west for five stormy days, to a place where he could build a new life for himself, his family, and his friends. A place where no other Vikings lived. A place where Erik would answer to no one but himself.

CHAPTER 2
Greenland

Greenland had been spotted by Vikings before. One Viking sighted this "bleak land of ice" while trying to reach Iceland. (Most of Greenland, the largest island in the world, lies north of the Arctic Circle.)

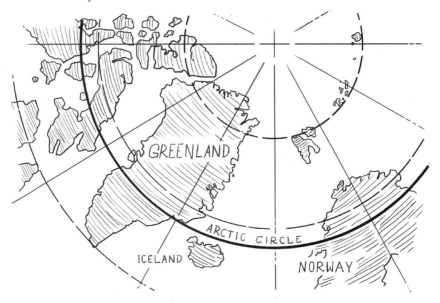

Another group of Vikings had once tried to establish a colony on an island off Greenland's coast. Within months, all the settlers were dead.

Erik the Red was determined to make life work on Greenland. The first place he and his small band of men landed was on the east coast of the island. It was very rocky and had few plants.

Cliffs plunged into the ocean. There were few places to land a ship. Inland, Erik spotted ice-covered mountains. He named this place Middle Glacier, and soon left. This was no place for a settlement.

Erik the Red and his men sailed on, rounding the southern tip of Greenland before continuing up along Greenland's west coast. Here, they found land that was better for their settlement: grassy fields to raise cows and sheep, and patches of land to farm. There were fjords (say: fee-YORDS) with deep, safe harbors to anchor a ship. And the water teemed with fish. On land, animals such as reindeer could be easily caught for food. The animals had never seen people before and weren't afraid.

Erik thought life could be good in Greenland. But it wouldn't be easy. Winters were bitter cold and very snowy. And while there was rich soil for farming, there wasn't much of it. Beyond the fjords and the green slopes that surrounded them, glaciers still covered most of the land.

Glaciers and Fjords

Glaciers are mountains of ice that form where there is lots of snow, and where the weather stays cold enough to keep the snow from melting. Layers of packed snow build into an icy glacier. As the glacier grows, it moves across the landscape.

Thousands of years before the Vikings, glaciers covered Scandinavia and Greenland. They cut deep, U-shaped valleys through the mountains as they grew and moved. At the end of the Ice Age, the glaciers began to melt, and the valleys filled with water. These beautiful, watery valleys are called fjords. Today there are more than one thousand fjords in Norway alone.

There was much hard work to be done. It would take many men to cut trees and build all the houses they would need. More families could help hunt and farm. Even though he himself hadn't been a very good one, Erik needed neighbors!

In the year 985, after three years of exploring, Erik returned to Iceland. He wanted to build his own Viking colony. To convince people to sail west with him, Erik decided to give his new land a nice-sounding name: Greenland. He made it sound as if the entire region was a beautiful, green landscape. What he *didn't* tell them was that there was more ice in Greenland than there was in Iceland!

Erik's plan worked: More than four hundred Icelanders decided to give Greenland a try. It was a dangerous journey. Twenty-five ships set sail, but only fourteen completed the voyage. Some were sunk, possibly by storms or icebergs; others were forced to return to Iceland.

Eventually, these newcomers arrived in
Greenland. They established a small village of
about two hundred farms near a place Erik had
named Eriksfjord, because it was "Erik's fjord."

It became known as the Eastern Settlement. Erik built his family a farm on Eriksfjord. He gave it the name Brattahlid (say: BRAH-tah-leed), which meant "steep slope."

Five-year-old Leif Erikson was home.

CHAPTER 3
Life of a Viking

Young Leif and the other Viking colonists enjoyed a pretty good life in the Eastern Settlement of Greenland.

They raised cattle, sheep, and goats on the grassy slopes and small fields. Butter and cheese were made from the animals' milk. Sheep's wool was used to produce cloth. Chickens roamed the Vikings' yards. Some settlers had traveled to Greenland with their pets, so dogs and cats now made their home in Greenland, too.

Like the Vikings back in Iceland and Scandinavia, those arriving in Greenland built homes called longhouses. A typical Viking longhouse was anywhere from 50 to 250 feet long,

about 20 feet wide, and made of one or two large rooms. To keep out the cold, longhouses usually had no windows.

At the center of the longhouse was the hearth, a fire pit that was almost always blazing. In Greenland, which was colder than Scandinavia, there might be more than one fireplace. Holes in the roof or chimneys allowed the smoke to escape. Fire provided warmth, light, and a way for the Vikings to cook their food.

Viking longhouses were typically made of wood, with a thick sod roof made of dirt and grass. But in Greenland, where there was less lumber, their homes were built with stone and peat—a brown, soil-like material made of dead and dry plants.

Vikings usually lived with their whole extended family. Grandparents, aunts, uncles, and cousins would all share space in the longhouse. Sometimes in the winter, the family's animals would be brought inside so they wouldn't freeze. The longhouse's walls were lined with benches, tables, and beds. A center aisle was kept clear, except for the hearth.

The hearth was not just the physical center of the home; it was also the center of Viking family life. After dinner, Vikings gathered around the fire to dance and sing, or to play board games.

In wealthy households, musicians and poets told fantastic tales of fierce battles and epic bravery. These stories were passed down from generation to generation beside roaring hearth fires on cold winter nights.

Three hundred miles up the coast from the Eastern Settlement, a second, smaller village was established. It was called the Western Settlement. From here, the Vikings were closer to the hunting grounds where they could find whales, polar bears, and seals. Walruses were highly prized for their ivory tusks.

The Viking Sagas

Long before Vikings could read and write, their history survived through storytelling. Warrior-poets known as skalds composed dramatic poems to describe the battles they had witnessed. The skalds used exciting language—for example, saying "battle sweat" to mean "blood"—to make their poems more memorable. Stories were also told about Viking families, both famous and ordinary—and about Viking mythology.

Around the year 1200, an Icelandic poet and politician named Snorri Sturluson began to write the stories down. Soon, others did, too. These became known as the Viking *sagas.*

Much of what we know about Leif Erikson and the Vikings comes from the sagas. But because the sagas were written hundreds of years *after*

Snorri Sturluson

the events took place, we can't be sure that all the details in the sagas are true. Even so, the Viking sagas are important sources in our understanding of Viking life.

Soon, the Greenlanders were trading their prized possessions, like whalebone crafts and polar-bear skins, with the Vikings in Norway and Ireland.

Erik the Red was the chieftain of the Greenland colony. The two settlements became successful. More Vikings moved there. Erik's people looked to him for guidance in all matters. The Thing was held at his family farm at Brattahlid. For fifteen years, Erik ran the colony as a fair and trusted chieftain.

Hot-tempered Erik the Red seemed to have finally calmed down. But he was often too busy running the settlement to be with his son Leif. Because of this, Leif Erikson spent much of his time with a man named Tyrkir.

Tyrkir helped raise Leif from the time he was a little boy. Leif thought of him as a foster father. As he grew up, Leif learned how to use a bow and arrow to hunt for reindeer and bears, and how to set traps to capture wild hares. He learned how to catch fish with barbed hooks and nets.

Leif was also taught about sailing and navigation. All good Viking boys, especially a son of a powerful chieftain like Erik the Red, had to learn their way around a boat.

Vikings were expert sailors who navigated the northern seas without compasses or nautical charts. So how did they know where they were going?

One way was by listening. The Vikings made up rhyming stories and songs that gave instructions for how to sail to certain places. These stories were passed down over the years from one generation of sailors to the next.

Vikings could also tell if they were close to land by listening closely for things like waves crashing on the shore, or by sniffing the air for trees or fire. They paid great attention to the natural world around them! If Viking sailors knew where certain animals, like a pod of whales, lived, they could use that information to figure out their own location.

Sometimes Viking sailors brought a bird on the ship with them. If they were out at sea and didn't know if they were close to land, they would release the bird. If the bird flew back to the ship later, that meant there was no land nearby.

The Vikings learned by observing and listening to nature's clues.

On clear days and nights, Viking sailors could use the position of the sun and the stars in the sky to determine where they were. On cloudy days, they may have used a small piece of clear

Sunstone

rock called a sunstone. It would be difficult to find the sun on days like these, but looking at the sky through a sunstone could have helped reveal the sun's true position.

Even with all their navigational know-how, the Vikings would never have been such successful sailors without their impressive ships.

The Viking boat, called a longship, was made from lightweight oak. The wooden planks overlapped one another and were held together with thousands of sturdy iron nails. Pine tar and

seal blubber (fat) were used to waterproof the wood. The oak was flexible, so it could bend without breaking, enabling the ship to shake and ripple with the waves. Along the bottom of the longship ran a finlike board called a keel. The keel prevented the ship from flipping over in choppy water.

Atop a forty-foot mast was attached a large, square sail that captured the wind to move the longship along at speeds of up to twenty-five miles per hour. If the wind died down, or if the Vikings simply wanted their ship to move faster, they pulled out long oars and started to row.

Viking longships were sturdy and strong, but light enough to be carried by their crew. They could sail the roughest seas, or float up narrow rivers and streams in as little as three feet of water.

Shaped like huge canoes, they could easily move backward or forward. They were, quite simply, the finest ships in the world.

There were two types of Viking ships: trading ships and warships.

Trading ships were about fifty feet long, and had two decks. Goods were stored belowdecks, while the crew worked above deck. This was the type of ship Erik the Red and his colonists had sailed from Iceland to Greenland.

Viking warships were called *drakhar*—or "dragon ships." Viking warriors decorated their *drakhar* with dragon's heads to strike fear in the hearts of their victims. Usually about seventy-five feet in length, the typical dragon ship held about

forty men—though some could fit a hundred.
The boats were flat, and so held no room below
deck for storage; the Viking warriors at sea lived
out in the open.

CHAPTER 4
The Viking Way of War

At home, the Vikings were farmers and hunters. Community and family life were important to them. But on the open sea, and on their summer raids, the Vikings were a force to be reckoned with. Expert sailors and fearless warriors, they knew what they wanted, and they did whatever it took to get it.

Young Leif Erikson came from a family with a tradition of violence and banishment. His father was known for his bad and murderous temper. So Leif Erikson, like all Vikings before him, had to learn how to fight. Viking warriors had a number of weapons in their collections.

Javelins were short spears thrown from a distance. Their barbed tips—curved into a small

Tyrkir teaching young Leif to fight

hook shape—would get caught in an enemy's shield. And because javelins were made of flexible steel, they bent and warped when they hit their targets. This made it harder for the javelin to be thrown back at the Viking warrior.

The Viking long spear, which could be up to six feet long, was probably the most common weapon. It was often thrown like the javelin.

Axes were also used in battle. A short ax was small enough to be held in one hand. The long ax—up to six feet in length—had to be held with two hands. Its twelve-inch blade could chop through an enemy's armor or split a helmet with a single swing.

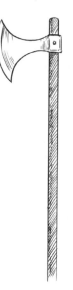

Swords were used by only the wealthiest Viking warriors. Their double-edged blades were made of iron, and their handles were often decorated with gold and silver. More common in a Viking's deadly toolkit was a long, single-bladed knife known as a sax. The sax could be used in battle— or at the dinner table!

For protection, Vikings carried brightly painted wooden shields. These lightweight shields sometimes came with straps attached, so they could be worn like backpacks when not in use.

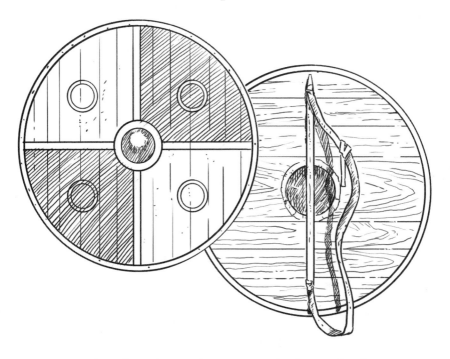

In battle, the Vikings used their shields to create a "shield wall." By interlocking their shields, they could protect themselves from flying arrows as they moved closer and closer to their enemy.

What's for Dinner?

The Vikings had a relatively rich and healthful diet. They ate meat every day—a boiled lamb or beef stew, or some bacon. They hunted animals from puffin to elk and fished quite a lot. Herring, which was plentiful, could be dried, pickled, salted, or smoked. Apples, nuts, and berries were collected from the woods, and vegetables like cabbage, peas, and beans were grown in gardens.

At the dinner table, Vikings ate from wooden bowls with a knife and a spoon, which was made of wood, bone, or antler. They drank beer from hollowed animal horns decorated with metal rims and tips. Bread almost always accompanied the meal.

Once the shield wall broke through the enemy's line, a second group of Vikings came in behind the shield wall, hacking away with their axes and swords. When the Vikings did battle, they preferred face-to-face, hand-to-hand combat. They considered the bow and arrow to be a cowardly weapon. They used it mostly for hunting.

For armor, Viking warriors probably wore vests and helmets made from leather, bone, or animal hide. Wealthier warriors might wear chain mail—shirts made of small interlinked metal rings. They also had metal helmets to protect their head, nose, and eyes. You might think that Viking raiders wore horned helmets. But, in fact, they never did!

Viking armor

Why the Horns?

The enduring image of the Viking in the horned helmet began in the 1800s, when Scandinavian artists began to paint Vikings wearing the headgear. In 1876, German composer Richard Wagner staged a four-part opera about the Norse gods and Viking myths. His costume designer dressed the performers in horned and feathered helmets. Opera was very influential at the time, and this iconic but inaccurate image of the Viking has stuck to this day.

From hunting to sailing to fighting, Leif Erikson learned from an early age what it took to be a Viking man. Like other Viking children, he did not attend school. Everything Leif learned—how to farm, how to start a fire—he learned from the grown-ups in his life.

One day, Leif Erikson—like his father and so many other Vikings before him—would sail off into the unknown. This sense of daring adventure was a part of who he was. It was the Viking way of life.

CHAPTER 5
The Viking Age

The Vikings had been sailing centuries before Leif Erikson's time. During the 700s, Vikings lived along the rocky coasts of Scandinavia. (They would not settle in Iceland for almost two hundred years.) Because the land surrounding them was so mountainous, Vikings used the seas and the fjords as their highways. They traded with their neighbors in Scandinavia and northern Europe.

During the summers, they raided. Like fearsome pirates, they pillaged and plundered foreign lands, bringing treasure and slaves back home with them.

The first recorded Viking raid took place in 793, in northeast England. The town of Lindisfarne was home to a Christian monastery that was full of valuable art and other treasures.

The Viking invaders descended on the monastery "like stinging hornets," and the holy men and women at Lindisfarne were not at all prepared.

The Vikings showed no mercy. According to records, they "robbed, tore, and slaughtered" everyone—priests and nuns alike. The church was "stripped of all its furnishing." The library was destroyed. Monks were taken as slaves, or drowned in the sea. Some people in England wondered if these fearsome warriors in their terrifying dragon ships had been sent by God to punish them. They had never seen anyone like the Vikings.

Almost two hundred years before Leif Erikson was born, the attack on Lindisfarne began what is known as the Viking Age.

The Vikings returned year after year to raid towns and monasteries up and down the English coast. They invaded the Orkney and Shetland Islands north of Scotland. Soon they had moved on to Ireland.

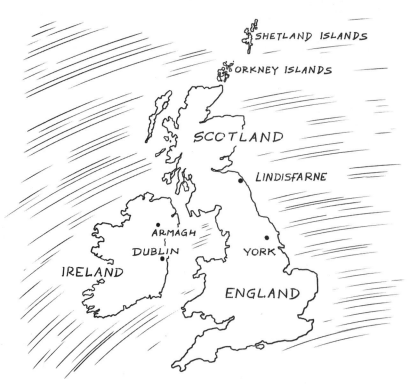

In 839, a fleet of more than one hundred Viking warships raided Armagh, Ireland's holiest city. A year later, they were back. Rather than return home, some Vikings decided to stay in Ireland. They sailed their longships up rivers to loot other holy cities. In 841, the Vikings established a trading port called Dublin, which today is Ireland's capital and largest city.

Most of these attacks were quick strikes against the locals. The Viking raiders went into a town or village, took what they wanted, and left. But, just as they had done in Ireland, some of the Vikings began to settle in the places they attacked.

Why?

Some historians believe that Scandinavia had become too crowded. With so little available farmland back home, the wide-open plains of the British Isles (England, Scotland, and Ireland) would have looked pretty inviting to the Viking invaders.

In 865, a massive army of Vikings invaded England. They marched inland to capture the walled city of York, destroying villages along the way. In the following years, they conquered much of the surrounding countryside. York became an

important Viking trading center and stronghold for the next hundred years.

The raids continued across Europe. The Vikings sailed their dragon ships up the rivers, reaching deep into the continent. In 845, they plundered Paris. After a payment of seven thousand pounds of silver from the locals,

the Vikings returned home. But the promise of more payments kept the Vikings coming back year after year. People learned to pay whatever they could scrape together to keep the Vikings *out* of their towns.

Vikings traveled as far as the Mediterranean Sea to raid cities in Spain and Italy—even North Africa!

While Viking women typically looked after the homestead, some joined the raids as doctors and cooks. They fixed broken weapons, sewed up nasty wounds, reset broken bones, and even amputated limbs! A few female warriors even fought alongside the men.

Trade also flourished during the Viking Age. Loaded with goods such as furs, timber, and ivory, Viking traders from Sweden did business as far away as Constantinople, capital of the Byzantine Empire, in present-day Turkey—a journey of about two thousand miles! They traded their stolen loot for the things they did not have, like silk and spices.

Viking traders reached Constantinople by sailing the rivers of Eastern Europe to the Black Sea. Along the way, they conquered cities like Kiev, the capital of modern-day Ukraine, and set up trading posts. Some historians believe that a tribe of Viking traders, called the "Rus," gave the country of Russia its name.

The Viking Age lasted for more than 250 years. During that time, Vikings in England and Ireland began to settle in with the local populations. Viking rulers began converting to Christianity, and their subjects followed suit. Around 954, the Viking king of England was kicked off the island. But in 1013, the Vikings returned and, for nearly thirty years, ruled England once again.

After being kicked out of England again, the king of Norway tried one last time to conquer England. He was killed in battle outside York. The year was 1066. The age of Viking rule outside Scandinavia was over for good.

Viking Words in English

The Vikings spoke a language called Old Norse. Many Norse words survive today in the modern English language. *Hūsbōndi* means "house occupier"—or *husband*. *Bǫrkr*, meaning "tree skin," became *bark* in English. *Happ*, Old Norse for "good fortune," turned into *happy*. And it would be a pretty unhappy and *rotten* birthday (*rotinn* meaning "decayed") without a birthday *kaka* ("cake")!

CHAPTER 6
The Road to Valhalla

By the year 1000, twenty-year-old Leif Erikson had grown up to be a tall and handsome man. On his way to visit the court of King Olaf in Norway, he stopped over in the Hebrides, a group of islands off the coast of Scotland. There, he met a beautiful noblewoman named Thorgunna.

Leif and Thorgunna had a son together, named Thorgils. Thorgunna remained in her homeland, but she later sent Thorgils to live with his father in Greenland. (Leif had another son, named Thorkell, back in Greenland. We do not know the name of Thorkell's mother.)

Leif Erikson left the Hebrides and continued on his journey to see Olaf, whose nickname was Crowbone. King Olaf had recently united Norway under one religion: Christianity. Olaf wanted Leif Erikson to convert his fellow Greenlanders to this religion, which was new to the Vikings.

For centuries, the Vikings had worshipped many different gods. In Christianity, there was only one true God. Leif Erikson wasn't so sure the Greenlanders would want to leave behind all the gods they'd grown up believing in.

But King Olaf didn't like to be told no. When Vikings in Iceland rejected the religion, King Olaf stopped trading with them. Without much-needed supplies coming to Iceland from Norway, the Icelanders soon changed their minds and converted!

Before their conversion to Christianity, the Vikings believed the universe was centered around one big tree: the World Tree. Atop this tree, an eagle perched, keeping a close eye on all corners of the world. Underground beneath the World Tree lay Nidhogg, a destructive dragon who chewed away at the tree's roots. A squirrel scampered up and down the World Tree, delivering insults between Nidhogg and the eagle.

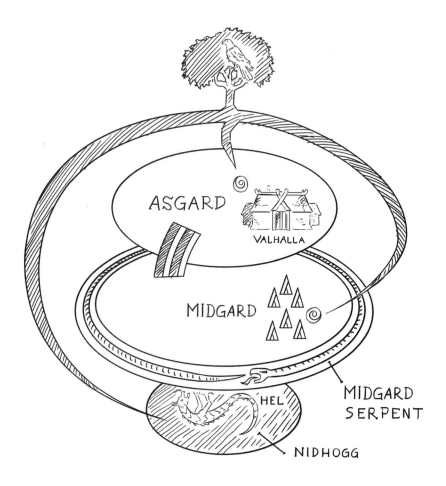

World Tree

At the top of the World Tree was Asgard, the home of the gods.

Odin was the one-eyed god of death, war, poetry, and wisdom—the king of all gods.

He rode an eight-legged horse, and Gungnir, his trusty spear, never missed its target.

Around the middle of the World Tree was a flat plane known as Midgard, or Middle Earth. This is where the humans lived—as well as giants, elves, and other magical creatures! Surrounding Middle Earth was the Midgard Serpent, a giant snake with a bite so poisonous, it could kill a god. Sail too far out to sea, the Vikings believed, and you might face this horrible beast.

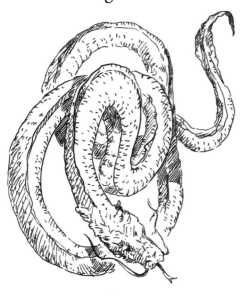

Deep underground, beneath the World Tree, was Hel: a land of rivers filled with blood and poison-spitting snakes! Hel was also the name of the evil goddess who ruled the underground realm.

Loki, Thor's foster brother, was the father to both Hel *and* the Midgard Serpent. Loki liked to play pranks. One time, one of Loki's jokes went too far and the god of light and justice ended up dead. Odin punished Loki by tying him to a rock in a cavern. The Vikings believed that earthquakes were caused by Loki struggling to break free of his shackles in the underworld.

Thor, Odin's son, was the god of storms and thunder. Thor killed giants in the sky with his massive hammer, causing the heavens to rumble with thunder and lightning.

Freya was the Norse goddess of beauty, love, and war. She decided who had babies, and who fell in love. She cried tears of gold after her husband, Od, disappeared. Her brother, Frey, was the god of good weather and good harvests.

Up in Asgard, all the gods had their own homes. Odin had three palaces. Valhalla was the one where Viking warriors who died bravely in battle would go in the afterlife.

After a battle, Odin's warrior angels—called the Valkyries—fetched the souls of the best fighters and flew them up to Valhalla on horseback. There, the warriors feasted in a great hall so large, you couldn't see from one end to the other. A rooftop of shields was propped up by strong spears. At the end of each nightly feast, the warriors went to sleep on benches covered in straw.

Every morning, they ran out to a battlefield, where they would fight one another to the death. They were training for the battle at Ragnarok,

the end of the world—the ultimate battle between good and evil. Each night after battle, the warriors were called in to feast. They picked up their chopped-off body parts, put themselves

back together, returned to the great hall, and did it all over again.

Fight. Feast. Repeat. This was the Vikings' idea of heaven!

Going Berserk

The legendary berserkers, or *Berserkir* (Norse for "bear shirt"), were a cult of fierce Viking warriors known to be absolutely vicious in battle. The night before a big battle, they would gather around a fire and drink mysterious teas that charged them up to fight. They wore the skins of wolves and bears into battle. They believed the spirits of these fearsome animals possessed them, along with the spirit of their god Odin.

When it was time to fight, these berserkers became wild with rage, biting chunks out of their wooden shields as they charged into battle. The berserkers were fearless fighters. They believed that if they died bravely in battle, they would be taken to Valhalla.

In real life, Vikings were devoted to their gods and the stories they believed about them. It's no wonder that Viking boys like Leif Erikson were raised to be so fearless. Theirs was a world of harsh realities, where you had to fight to survive. To live a glorious afterlife in the great halls of Valhalla, you must live your life on Earth as a dedicated warrior.

But Leif knew what he had to do for the Vikings of Greenland. He became a Christian. He promised King Olaf that when he returned home, he would spread the word of God among his fellow Greenlanders by bringing Christian missionaries with him.

King Olaf was pleased.

Though many Vikings had already abandoned their old Norse gods, one Viking did *not* give up his old beliefs. Erik the Red, the sagas say, became "greatly annoyed" when Leif's mother became a Christian.

Still, to please his wife and his son, Erik agreed that a small church would be built on the family farm at Brattahlid. The church was tiny, about six feet wide and eleven feet long, but it could hold about twenty-five Vikings.

CHAPTER 7
Voyage to Vinland

Having converted the Greenland Vikings to Christianity, Leif Erikson set about his next mission: to explore the unknown western lands that Bjarni Herjólfsson had spotted so many years earlier. Perhaps Leif could build a settlement across the sea, just as his father had done in Greenland.

Leif visited Bjarni, who told Leif which way to sail, then sold him his ship. Next, Leif gathered a crew of thirty-four men to join him on his voyage, including his foster-father and friend, Tyrkir.

Leif also asked his father, Erik, to lead the expedition. Now about fifty years old, Erik the Red was much older than he had been when founding the Viking settlements on Greenland. But Erik agreed to join anyway.

Leif and his crew prepared their ship to set sail. Soon it was summer—and time to leave. Erik the Red rode his horse down from the farm at Brattahlid. Along the way, the horse stumbled, and Erik was badly injured.

"This is as far as we go together," Erik told his son. Leif would have to lead the historic expedition himself.

Leif and his crew sailed down the fjord and out into the open sea. Following Bjarni's directions, they traveled up Greenland's coast before making a sharp turn west into the open sea. After several days, they spotted land. Leif anchored the ship.

He and some crewmembers rowed to shore on a small boat.

The land was bleak and without much life at all. Pounding waves crashed into tall seaside cliffs. Leif found no grass, only rock and ice. It was unsuitable land for a settlement. Leif named the place Helluland, meaning "land of flat stones." Today, it is known as Canada's Baffin Island.

Leif Erikson had reached North America!

The men sailed south from Helluland. A few days later, they spotted a land of thick woods and white sand. Once again, they dropped anchor and went ashore to explore. The Vikings were amazed by the area's huge beaches—up to two hundred feet wide!—and dense seaside forests. Leif named this place Markland, meaning "wood land." Still, Leif found little grass. It was not a good spot to raise livestock. Leif and his men rowed back to their ship and sailed on.

A few days later, Leif spotted a strait—a waterway between two pieces of land. He turned the ship into the strait, then landed their boat on a small island just north of modern-day Newfoundland.

Here, at last, Leif saw fields of thick grass, heavy with dew. Leif and his men got down on the ground and drank the water droplets from the grass. After so long on a boat, the fresh water tasted sweet to everyone! But the island was too small for a settlement. So Leif continued on his way.

Soon, Leif steered the ship into a river that emptied into the bay. It led directly to a clear lake full of fish. The surrounding area was lush and green and full of life. The weather was warm, and this far south—farther south than Leif had ever been—the days lasted longer than they did in Greenland.

Leif decided to spend the winter in this wonderful new place. They cut down trees and built a lumberyard. Houses were constructed using thick slabs of turf—a mat of soil, grass, and plant roots. A dock was built so Leif and his men could make repairs to their ship.

Every day, Leif sent half his crew to go out exploring. Leif's orders were to return to camp before nightfall. One night, Tyrkir didn't come back.

Fearing the worst, Leif gathered a dozen men to go out searching for his foster-father. They didn't get far before they ran into Tyrkir, who was running toward them. He was excited. "I have a real novelty to report," he told Leif. "I have found vines and grapes."

Grapes could be made into wine. And no grapes grew back in Greenland. Leif was very pleased with Tyrkir's discovery! He named the region Vinland, meaning "wine land."

All winter long, Leif and his men collected grapes and chopped down trees. There was little lumber back home, and certainly no grapes! Best of all, no snow fell all season long. The next spring, they loaded their ship and set sail back to Greenland.

Along the way, Leif spotted a chain of rocks, called a reef, poking out of the water. As he sailed closer, he noticed a group of fifteen men standing on the rocks, shouting and waving. Their ship had struck the reef and sunk. They were stranded. Leif welcomed them aboard the ship.

From that day forward, Leif Erikson became known as Leif the Lucky.

Soon after Leif returned home to Greenland, Erik the Red died. Leif became the new chieftain of his people. From the family farm at Brattahlid, he ruled Greenland with his sons Thorgils and Thorkell by his side.

Leif Erikson was chieftain of Greenland for more than twenty years. He continued to preach Christianity to his people. Under Leif's rule, the colony grew and prospered.

Leif never returned to Vinland. Around the year 1025—nobody knows precisely how or when—Leif Erikson died. His son Thorkell ruled Greenland after his death. But Leif Erikson's brave and adventurous legacy lived on.

CHAPTER 8
The Vikings and the Skraelings

Leif never sailed back to North America, but other Vikings did—including his two brothers and sister.

Leif's brother Thorvald Erikson led the first expedition back to Vinland. Thorvald and a crew of about thirty men spent two winters at Leif's old camp, cutting down trees and grapevines.

Thorvald then set off to explore the area further. He sailed up a long fjord to a pleasant wooded area.

Thorvald decided he would like to build a home here. However, on the sand, Thorvald and his crew noticed three strange mounds. They were canoes, and under each one hid three men. This was already someone else's home.

Immediately, Thorvald and his men attacked, killing eight of the nine native men.

Only one of the Native Americans, whom the Vikings called Skraelings (say: SKRAY-uh-lings), escaped and ran to tell his tribe about the murderous invaders. The Skraelings returned and surrounded the Vikings. As Thorvald and his men ran back to their ship, arrows rained down upon them. Thorvald was struck, and he later died.

After the Skraelings had left the area, Thorvald's crew buried him in the spot where he had wished to build his home in Vinland. The Vikings stayed in North America for one more season before returning to Greenland.

Upon hearing of his brother's death, Leif's other brother, Thorstein, decided to sail to Vinland to bring Thorvald's body back to be buried in Greenland. But wild storms prevented him from completing his journey. Thorstein's ship returned to Greenland without ever making it to North America.

A Viking trader named Thorfinn Karlsefni led the next trip from Greenland to Vinland. About 130 people, including Karlsefni's wife, joined the expedition. Karlsefni also brought along cows and sheep. He planned to make the Viking settlement in North America a permanent one.

For three winters, Karlsefni and his fellow explorers lived in Vinland. As on previous

expeditions, the Vikings gathered lumber and grapes. Karlsefni's wife gave birth to a son named Snorri—the first European to be born in North America.

The Native Americans returned to the Viking camp, this time to trade skins for cow's milk and red cloth. But what they really wanted was the settlers' iron weapons. When one Skraeling was caught trying to steal weapons, he was killed on the spot.

Karlsefni feared a war would break out between the Vikings and the natives, so he decided to return to Greenland with the valuable cargo of lumber and grapes they had collected.

The voyage of Leif's sister, Freydis, was the last attempt to build a permanent settlement of Greenlanders in North America. Unlike previous expeditions, Skraelings attacked Freydis's crew almost immediately after they arrived in Vinland. According to one of the Viking sagas, Freydis—who was pregnant at the time—lifted a sword from one of her dead countrymen, held it up to the approaching Skraelings, and dared them to attack her. The Skraelings turned around.

Although she was brave, Freydis realized the Vikings were greatly outnumbered by the Skraelings. They quickly returned to Greenland. The dream of a permanent colony in Vinland was over.

Where Is Vinland?

In 1960, a Viking settlement was discovered at the northern tip of Newfoundland, Canada. The site, which was dated to around the year 1000, was given the name L'Anse aux Meadows—the Cove of Meadows.

There was evidence of eight buildings at L'Anse aux Meadows. One building included a furnace for producing iron—technology that the Native

Americans at the time did not have. But there were also remains of butternuts, a type of walnut that grew in forests hundreds of miles away, in other parts of Canada: New Brunswick, Quebec, and Nova Scotia.

So did the Vikings travel even farther into North America? Probably so. The sagas mention multiple settlements in Vinland. But to date, no real evidence of Viking settlements has been found anywhere besides what is now Newfoundland.

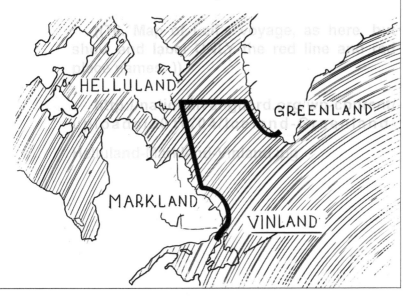

CHAPTER 9
Life After Leif

Back in Greenland, the Viking colony continued to grow after the death of Leif Erikson, as more Vikings from Iceland—and later from Norway—moved there. The Greenlanders traded walrus-tusk ivory and other goods with Europeans. At the colony's height, as many as 3,500 people lived in Greenland. But after about 450 years, the Greenland settlements disappeared.

Why?

A major factor was the long-term weather patterns in Greenland.

When Erik the Red settled Greenland in the late 900s, the climate was warmer. There were fewer icebergs, so the Vikings could sail easily into port and out to sea to hunt for whales and seals.

By the 1300s, the weather in Europe and the North Atlantic had grown colder and stormier. Thick sea ice returned. Hunting and trading expeditions became dangerous—or even impossible. Crops failed. And the Vikings abandoned Greenland.

While the Greenlanders likely never returned to Vinland after their failed attempts at colonization, they had continued sailing to Markland to cut down timber. But eventually, the way to Vinland was forgotten. It seemed like no more than a legend.

On July 4, 1825, long after the Viking Age had ended and Greenland was abandoned, six families in Norway boarded a ship called *Restauration*. Like their ancestor Leif Erikson, they were bound for North America. These fifty-two people became the first organized group of Norwegian immigrants to settle in the United States. Many more would follow in their footsteps.

One hundred years later, President Calvin Coolidge addressed a crowd of more than eighty thousand Norwegian Americans in Minnesota. In his speech, the president acknowledged what the crowd knew to be true: that Leif Erikson had explored America centuries before Christopher

Columbus. The crowd roared its approval with pride.

In 1929, the state of Wisconsin declared October 9—the day *Restauration* reached New York Harbor—to be Leif Erikson Day. Soon, other states did the same. In 1964, the United States Congress made Leif Erikson Day official nationwide.

Leif Erikson Day the SpongeBob Way

Leif Erikson Day is one of cartoon character SpongeBob SquarePants's favorite holidays! In the episode called "Bubble Buddy," SpongeBob rises early to wish his best friend, Patrick, a "Happy Leif Erikson Day." Wearing a fake red beard and metal helmet, he calls out "Hinga Dinga Durgen!"—the official greeting of the holiday in Bikini Bottom.

Today, millions of Americans trace their heritage back to Scandinavia. Most of them live in the Midwest, where many cheer on their favorite football team, the Minnesota Vikings.

Statues honoring Leif Erikson stand in public parks from Seattle to North Dakota to Boston.

While he was never able to establish a permanent settlement in Vinland, Leif the Lucky was indeed the first European to explore the North American continent. A skilled sailor and brave leader, Leif Erikson didn't let the old Norse legends of his father and their Viking ancestors keep him from discovering the unknown parts of the world. His voyage motivated others to follow in his path, and continues to inspire people today.

Seattle's Leif Erikson statue

Timeline of the Vikings, Erik the Red, and Leif Erikson

793	Vikings attack Lindisfarne; Viking Age begins
841	Vikings establish trading port at Dublin, Ireland
c. 880	Harald Fairhair unites Norway
960	Erik the Red and his father are banished from Norway and move to Iceland
c. 980	Leif Erikson born in Iceland
982	Erik the Red banished from Iceland, sails to Greenland
985	Leif moves to Greenland
	First Viking settlements established in Greenland
986	Bjarni Herjólfsson first sees unknown lands to the west of Greenland
1000	Leif visits King Olaf in Norway; agrees to convert Greenlanders to Christianity
	Leif discovers Vinland
c. 1003	Erik the Red dies; Leif becomes chieftain of Greenland
c. 1025	Leif Erikson dies
1066	King Harald III of Norway attempts to invade England and is defeated; Viking Age ends
c. 1450	Vikings abandon Greenland
1964	US Congress establishes October 9 as Leif Erikson Day

Timeline of the World

794	In Japan, the city of Heian (later called Kyoto) founded
843	Treaty of Verdun divides the Carolingian Empire (which covers most of Italy, France, and Germany) into three kingdoms
852	First parachute is used in Córdoba, Spain
868	Oldest known book in the world, the *Diamond Sutra*, is printed in northern China
960	Sung Dynasty, a period of artistic development and economic growth, begins in China
c. 970	First university in the world is founded in Cairo, Egypt
c. 1010	World's first novel, *The Tale of Genji*, written by a woman in Japan
1024	Bolesław the Brave becomes the first king of Poland
1040	Duncan, king of Scotland, is killed by his cousin Macbeth
1429	Joan of Arc frees Orleans, France, from the English
1450	Johannes Gutenberg invents the printing press in Germany
1492	Christopher Columbus sails to the West Indies, the first European explorer to do so
1607	William Shakespeare completes his play *Macbeth*
1969	Neil Armstrong becomes the first person to walk on the moon

Bibliography

*Books for young readers

*D'Aulaire, Ingri, and Edgar Parin D'Aulaire. ***D'Aulaires' Book of Norse Myths.*** New York: New York Review Children's Collection, 1967.

Ferguson, Robert. ***The Vikings.*** New York: Penguin Books, 2010.

*Knudsen, Shannon. ***Leif Eriksson.*** Minneapolis, MN: Millbrook Press, 2005.

Lewis, Richard S. ***From Vinland to Mars: A Thousand Years of Exploration.*** New York: Quadrangle Books, 1976.

Lilley, Harvey, director. ***NOVA: Vikings Unearthed.*** A BBC Production with PBS, NOVA/WGBH Boston, and France Television, 2016.

Marcus, G. J. ***The Conquest of the North Atlantic.*** Woodbridge, Suffolk, England: Boydell Press, 1980.

*Thompson, Ben. ***Guts and Glory: The Vikings.*** New York: Little, Brown and Company, 2015.